D1172888

DON'TS
FOR WEDDINGS

A. & C. BLACK, LTD.
LONDON

PREFACE

Love should be the Lord of Marriage.
True happiness cannot exist without
it, however great the wealth or exalted
the position of the married pair. The
worst evils of life are made bearable
by its presence. Only a passion based
on selfishness will plunge the beloved
into despair and privation. True love
has a substratum of common sense, self-
restraint, and thought for others.

There are those who say that mutual
respect and sufficient means are the
only reliable things with which to enter
upon matrimony. Both are compatible
with love, in fact respect must be part

of the softer passion or it will not wear well. No one will deny that a marriage founded on mere respect may one day be crowned by lasting love; nor that pre-matrimonial love may die a speedy death soon after the couple is united. These possibilities don't alter the fact that Love is the most precious asset with which to begin married life.

ANON

DON'TS FOR WEDDINGS

I.—*CHOOSING A SPOUSE.*

DON'T single out a girl if you don't intend to propose to her.

Don't eschew possibilities for an informal introduction. Rescue her dog from a street fray, pick up a trinket she has dropped, or travel with her on a long journey and prove yourself her cavalier.

Don't despair if you are a lady and seek an entrée to a particular man. Confide in your brother or married lady friend. Either will seek an introduction without giving you away.

Don't permit girls to form foolish ideas about men. A girl with brothers or men friends will make a wiser choice than one who has formed her ideas from heroes of fiction.

Don't haunt a girl whose acquaintance you seek. There is a wide margin between accepting invitations in the hope of meeting her and walking past her house several times a day, or shadowing her in public places.

Don't assume to marry your first love, for matrimony demands as much special attention as the learned professions. Unqualified amateurs swell the lists of the divorce court.

Don't spurn the suitor with some experience of women and their ways. He makes a better lover than one who is ignorant.

Don't discourage the girl in her teens who offers her love ; she may find full satisfaction in matrimony. Blind self-confidence and impulsive inexperience may though lay up sorrows for the future. Don't hurry a young girl into marriage.

Don't rule out the boy or girl you grew up with. You may wake one day to find a new shyness between you, to be dispelled by fuller, sweeter comradeship.

Don't forget that other men will supply your deficiencies if you are negligent.

Don't discount the power of existing friendship, as you know the tastes and weaknesses, temperament and surroundings of the woman you have chosen.

Don't be surprised if love awakens during a separation, or when a rival appears.

II.—*THE COURTSHIP*.

Don't belittle the delicious insecurity preceding a Declaration of Love. It may be the ante-chamber to an earthly paradise. It may be a fool's paradise.

Don't force yourself upon her if your attentions are unwelcome. You have no right if she has used every means, short of rudeness, to show she does not desire your nearer acquaintance.

Don't, till you have declared yourself, object to her receiving attentions from anyone else. You have no say over her favours, nor can you put a spoke in another man's wheel.

Don't send gifts other than flowers, bon-bons, and pretty trifles till you have confessed your love. You may give her a dog or kitten, or the undressed skin of an animal you have shot, but you must not offer articles of jewellery, furs, or items of toilette.

Don't forget to enclose a little note in offering a present while your love remains unconfessed.

Don't startle the lady of your heart by too sudden a development. Some women like to be taken by storm, but most girls like to enjoy being wooed and won.

Don't forget to allow a short interval once you have permission to call. Wait just long enough to give the lady time to think about you and long for your coming.

Don't transgress etiquette in your first call, but leave with a pretext for a less formal visit. Convey to your lady that the sun will not shine till you see her again.

Don't single out your girl from the rest of her people and invite her alone. Until there is an acknowledged engagement, her parent, brother, or sister should be included.

Don't neglect to discover what interests her people. Bring her father cuttings for the garden. Lend her mother books, sing or recite at her charity entertainments.

Don't expect a nice-minded girl to tolerate a man who is discourteous to her parents—however flattering his attitude to herself.

Don't wonder that free and easy parents often find their daughters remain unmarried. Man is a hunter who values his spoils in proportion to the difficulties overcome in the chase.

Don't hesitate to introduce your chosen one to your own womenkind. Say that your mother and sister would so much like to call. Unless there is some feminine feud, permission will be cordially given.

Don't discount your sister who may discreetly play the part of Number Three. Your brother can bring your man home to dinner, or arrange cycling expeditions.

Don't forget that married friends may afford delightful opportunities of meeting. Where it is possible and convenient, you may arrive and leave together.

Don't monopolise a man whose profession keeps him from home for long intervals. Don't be piqued if he has to take his sister out, or spend the evening with his parents. He will be the better husband for such courtesies.

Don't hesitate to invite the man who lives in rooms to drop in as he likes—he misses the delights of home. He will come on Sunday afternoons, and end by staying to supper.

Don't overlook the workings of the
household of a lady with domestic
responsibilities. Don't look aggrieved if
she cannot go cycling with you because
she has promised to take the little ones
blackberrying. Seize a golden chance
and go with them.

Don't scorn a bachelor girl who is
living in independent fashion. It may
prove interesting to divert her from
anti-matrimonial theories.

Don't abuse your love's modesty.
See your lady home in the evening, but
don't smoke in her flat till the small
hours.

Don't discount a lady in business whose schedule is regular ; you will know where to find her. If you are employed in the same firm, you have daily chances of rendering her small services.

Don't get her into hot water by hindering her at work.

Don't display the buttonhole he bought you to the other girls, nor give yourself away by hanging about his room door. Find time for a word or bright glance when you do meet, by accident of course.

Don't make her conspicuous by always travelling home together, but be at hand to pilot her through a fog or help her out of a crowd.

Don't propose what you know to be beyond his means, when you plan a Saturday outing. You may pardon him for a little extravagance in your honour.

Don't take her to a place of amusement where she would feel out of her element, or risk a snub. A girl earning thirty shillings in your father's office will feel more at home on the river than at the Carlton.

Don't believe that because a man is an artist he must lack courtesy to women. Likewise, it is not inevitable that a girl with a talent for drawing should violate all the proprieties.

Don't omit to encourage your chosen man. Wear his flowers, and let him see that you have kept the best in water after the dance.

Don't bestow effusive attentions on your lover, nor boast of his devotion to you. It is good for him to see that other men are in the running.

Don't try to detach your lover from the rest of the company, though you both enjoy a *tête-à-tête*. Don't seek fictitious errands to the bottom of the garden. Leave him to find the opportunities.

III.—*THE QUESTION OF AGE.*

Don't approach marriage in early youth. A child-wife of seventeen and a boy of twenty will most likely rue their folly before they reach maturity.

Don't put off matrimony unto middle-age without good reason. The woman of thirty-eight and the man of forty-five will spoil their children while they are little, and be out of touch with them as they grow up.

Don't discourage a match between a girl of two- or three-and-twenty and a man of twenty-eight or thirty. This is an ideal union of vigour, looks and experience.

Don't moralise over young lovers. We smile at their rapturous happiness, yawn over their ecstasies ; we know they are passing through a phase, and make excuses.

Don't deny later problems if you marry a man much younger than yourself. The advance of age will make you old while he remains in his prime. You may pray for death for release, or wear a wig and paint your face, but if you live long enough, both of you will suffer.

Don't scoff at the older man who retains youth's vitality ; many a girl would be proud to marry him.

Don't disregard that an older unmarried man will have a very good or very bad reason for being single.

Don't buy a young wife from selfish motives, or you may lose by the bargain.

Don't enter courtship in maturity without self-restraint and dignity. It is bad taste to gush over your lover, coquetting like a kitten, telling the world how you rejoice.

Don't adorn your mature love with white muslin and blue ribbons ; show your joy in nice gowns and dainty lace.

Don't trifle with your middle-aged *fiancée* by neglecting her for younger, fresher faces. Ease her burdens, and give her credit for managing so far to get through life without you.

IV.—*THE PROPOSAL.*

Don't make an offer of marriage till you are in a position to support a wife. No lady should waste her youth nor heart on a man who is not trying to make their marriage possible.

Don't choose a ring unless it is the best you can afford, and the right fit. Seek out one of special design ; one good stone is better than several smaller ones.

Don't make your first request to the lady's parents ; this is bygone etiquette.

Don't propose when a servant is due to arrive with a scuttle of coals, nor when the children are tumbling in from school. Your declaration is not likely to meet with favour.

Don't despair if you lack moonlight or the stillness of a summer's eve. A man of tact will know how to speak in sweetest cadences.

Don't make a verbal offer if you are nervous or unready. You had much better write it in a letter, and then be intelligible.

Don't succumb to an Unwelcome Offer. You may save the situation by a timely jest—not at his expense.

Don't run the risk of an inopportune proposal. Keep a child at your side, or linger with the greatest bore. Don't go for moonlit strolls or gaze at the stars on board ship.

Don't marry in haste. To meet one week and propose the next is a doubtful compliment.

Don't fail to ensure your lady understands that you are asking her to be your wife—she cannot urge you to be explicit.

Don't say Yes merely because you are tired of saying No.

Don't reject rudely, unkindly, or with scorn any honourable offer of marriage.

Don't keep a man in suspense while you angle for a better matrimonial prize.

Don't reject his offer with rudeness ; it is best to appear unsympathetic.

Don't stoop to asking a man to marry you ; there is something repellent in a marriage offer coming from a woman's lips.

Don't avail yourself of the supposed privilege of Leap Year.

Don't desist, if you are wealthy, from the man of your choice. Lesser men will woo you for your banking account, but if you see him held back by moral qualms, let love melt the golden barrier between you.

Don't resent being closely questioned before your reception into a family. Be ready to give all particulars that may be required.

Don't omit to state what your income and prospects are, the probable date at which you will be able to marry, and how you intend to provide for your wife.

Don't discourage her father's confidence—there are some warnings that must be heeded, notably where there is taint of insanity within the family.

Don't display unseemly curiosity as to your bride's marriage portion. Most fathers state plainly how their daughters will be dowered, unless they suspect you of mercenary motives.

Don't, where consent is refused, try to force your way into a family. Abide by the decision and remain true. Time may enable a more successful attempt.

V.—*CELEBRATING THE ENGAGEMENT.*

Don't tarry once the engagement is settled. A few days later, the lady's parents should give a dinner for close friends, or a larger At Home.

Don't omit to tell friends at a distance : the lady's mother will write to inform her friends, and the *fiancée* will spread the news to her own chums. The man tells his own people and friends of his good fortune.

Don't offer good wishes to the couple without a warm clasp of the hand and a few heartfelt words.

Don't display your alarm in offering congratulations, if your friend has chosen oddly.

Don't fail to congratulate *him*, even though she is worlds too good for him ; what to say to *her* when you feel she is making a disastrous match is a painful problem.

Don't deny her your wish that her brightest dreams be realised, even where you have little hope of it. Show no bitterness in your congratulations.

VI.—*THE ENGAGED COUPLE.*

Don't ignore that your relatives may not welcome your bride-elect. She must bear herself simply and naturally under criticism.

Don't parade your power over your lover in his own home—or anywhere else, for the matter of that.

Don't be foolish and pretend that you don't care for him, or talk of your wedding-day as if it were your execution.

Don't devote yourself exclusively to him, and fail in courtesy to his family or their friends.

Don't boast of your own people, or infer that your home is superior to theirs.

Don't show any wish to oust your lover's mother from her place in his affections. Women are always jealous of the girls their sons marry ; take care to disarm this.

Don't spend fewer than two or three evenings a week at her home. Dine there on Sundays, and, if you are busy all week, devote Saturday afternoons to her entirely.

Don't make vulgar exhibition of your love : a close clasp of the hand or silent greeting of the eyes will suffice.

Don't tyrannise your *fiancé*. If you order him about and take his submission as your due, rest assured that one day the worm will surely turn.

Don't shirk in sacrificing yourselves when out. You may see that she has all she wants at a garden party or At Home, but don't glare at another man for handing her a cup of tea.

Don't attract attention by devoting yourself to any other lady, or by playing into the hands of a wanton flirt.

Don't give yourself away by allowing awkward pauses in conversation because your eyes are hungrily following your lover.

Don't make yourself conspicuous in your behaviour with any other admirer, but be at ease with any man with whom you may have occasion to speak.

Don't consider the cosy corners, shady walks, and secluded nooks your monopoly at a house-party. Exercise a little healthful self-control.

Don't neglect to go about together as much as possible in *tête-à-tête* intercourse. Lovers must learn to pass their lives together.

Don't fail to take little expeditions together. You may otherwise mar your honeymoon by feeling shy or strange.

Don't always pay expenses when you take your sweetheart about. Share the costs if you are of moderate means and your *fiancée* has an allowance.

Don't make a rule of writing to each other at bedtime with all you had not time to say, having parted only at 7 P.M. It may become a tax, and breaking it on either side may cause pain and friction.

Don't belittle love-letters when daily or frequent meetings are impossible. They have an important part to play in the course of true love.

Don't reveal to anyone the secrets of your exchange. Your letters must remain private. To you they will be sublime ; to the outsider they would be ridiculous.

Don't rush an engagement. Let it be long enough for your love to settle into a more normal state, where you can gain a clearer estimate of your mutual fitness.

Don't risk criticism by urging a hasty marriage if you are a lady. Let that come from your *fiancé*.

VII.—*SHOULD MATTERS GO AWRY.*

Don't hesitate to ask your parents to speak to him if he lets time drag on. If you guess that he has no real desire to marry, best give him up than urge him to take the step unwillingly.

Don't begrudge your man his freedom, if your union is set to fail. Release him before he has to ask for it.

Don't openly and wantonly disregard your man's wishes on any important point : his self-respect will otherwise require to break with you.

Don't permit your *fiancé* to continue bad habits, such as gambling, intemperance, or similar sins. Let him choose between you and his vices.

Don't continue with wedding plans if you have idealised your lady, been blinded by her beauty or bedazzled by her wit. Consider the woman as she really is.

Don't despair if you change your mind. The cause is most likely the advent of the right woman.

Don't neglect to send back the ring and other tokens should your engagement be broken. Burn letters or return them to the writer – feelings run strong over written proofs of a love that has disappointed.

VIII.—*ELOPEMENTS.*

Don't be deterred from making your own choice when you are of age if your parents object to your lover for his poverty, or some personal prejudice.

Don't overlook that you face misery and disgrace if you bind yourself to a man whose moral unfitness is manifest.

Don't accept other suitors who may be urged upon you. Rest true to him you love till you are free to give your hand in marriage.

Don't resist making a confidante of your mother if she is sympathetic, and your father a Spartan. Your mother will seek your happiness.

Don't bind a girl to yourself by marriage if you have no prospects to offer, then return her home as if nothing had happened.

Don't marry in secret for fear of losing money if you reveal the truth. Love is not enough without the wherewithal to gild it.

Don't stain the outset of your wedded life with deception and falsehood. So are sown the seeds of distrust and contempt where love and trust should flourish.

IX.—*PREPARATIONS, GOWNS AND THE TROUSSEAU.*

Don't put off naming the day, once your engagement has served its purpose. Once the groom's finances are secure, and the bride is willing to renounce freedom for bonds that should be blessed, you may proceed to the marriage.

Don't fix a date in May, which is considered unlucky for weddings : "If married in Lent / You are sure to repent."

Don't hasten but allow a good interval between the final decision and the day itself. At least a month or six weeks is suitable ; more allows due time for preparations.

Don't rush at the last but prepare calmly for the most vital step in your life. Ensure you both have some days of peace to ponder the gravity of your new responsibilities.

Don't hurry the bride-elect from milliner to dressmaker, jeweller to shoemaker, furrier to glovemaker, day in day out. She will otherwise be kept in a whirl of excitement till she is well-nigh worn out.

Don't permit the choice of bridesmaids to become a source of family friction. The bride's sisters must take precedence, then her dearest schoolfriend. Finally, *his* sisters must be asked ; they may be neither attractive nor young.

Don't discount forswearing all adults in favour of two or three children—a prettier and less expensive arrangement.

Don't ignore your future social position—avoid selecting a magnificent satin dinner-gown with a court train if you are marrying a man with a small income.

Don't weigh yourself down with unbecoming brocades and stiff silks. Your sweetness and beauty will look the fresher in soft, diaphanous fabrics, which fall into graceful draperies.

Don't ignore the comfort and fit of your bridal frock, shoes and gloves, and the set of your veil. Don't be handicapped by pinching garments on your wedding-day !

Don't misjudge costumes for the bridesmaids. White may suit two of the sisters, but prove trying to the complexion of another. Consider also the height and build of the various girls. This is a matter demanding much tact and delicacy.

Don't expect your bridesmaids to buy extravagant hats and frocks, which may be of little use afterwards. They may otherwise be obliged to decline to attend you at the altar.

Don't forget that elderly bridesmaids in youthful frocks and girlish hats are ridiculous to the unthinking, and pathetic to those who look beneath the surface.

Don't permit one bridesmaid to have her frock made by an artiste ; the others must follow suit or the picture will be spoilt.

Don't, if marrying in your travelling dress, allow your attendants to wear dresses that eclipse your own.

Don't choose a dainty creation for your travelling dress if you have hard travelling ahead with your husband ; it should be tailor-made, stylish and devoid of fallals.

Don't discount season with regard to your materials. White gauzy frocks look chill in mid-winter, and may afflict the wearers with red noses.

Don't underestimate the value of a few gowns of good material and excellent cut. Few people buy many dresses at once, on account of the changeful whims of fashion.

Don't omit the necessities. It is a disgrace to don a fine opera-cloak if you have no decent dressing-gown.

Don't forget the value of quality ; a good cloth is more important than the trimmings and make. It is good economy to buy the best where regular or hard wear is required.

X.—*THE INVITATIONS.*

Don't overcomplicate invitations to the wedding. Choose a design that is simple and refined from any good stationer.

Don't neglect to invite any friend who has sent a present before the invitations are out.

Don't reject the notion of only asking friends to the church ; you are entitled to confine the reception at home to members of the two families.

Don't feel obliged to offer a present in return for an invitation—it takes away from the voluntary spirit of a gift.

Don't omit to invite a bridesmaid who lives at a distance to stay at the bride's home for a few days before the wedding.

XI.—*WEDDING PRESENTS.*

Don't seek to promote your own social ambition through your gift. There is much vulgar advertisement over private weddings.

Don't follow convention in your choice of wedding present. Mustard-pots and salt-cellars are monotonous ; private friends may exercise greater invention.

Don't discount offering a cheque. This is perfectly acceptable if you are an old friend or relation of the happy couple.

Don't offer silver if the bride will have only one servant. She will have to rub up her own brushes and sweet-meat dishes.

Don't pass up the opportunity, if you don't feel kindly towards the man or woman to whom your friend is affianced, to send a gift that will be a pleasure only to your friend—not a mustard-pot into which both will dip the spoon!

Don't fail, promptly and personally, to acknowledge all gifts sent to you.

Don't, if your wedding present is sent from the shop direct, fail to enclose your card. Many people fix on their cards with narrow white ribbon.

Don't choose a present just because you like the object yourself. A grand piano is no good to those who will not have a large room.

XII.—*SETTING UP HOME.*

Don't, where possible, start married life together other than in a home of your own.

Don't miss the sweetness of home-hunting expeditions, even taking into account the misleading tactics of the house agent.

Don't spurn any financial help offered by your bride's father.

Don't trust your groom to superintend the choice of your home. Check provision of cupboards and store-rooms, the aspect of the larder and condition of the kitchen range.

Don't object to visiting the abode with a practised housewife if you are young and inexperienced in household management.

Don't shy from consulting your groom's mother about domestic details. It will please her greatly and you will profit by her valuable advice.

Don't furnish your home fully till after the wedding. A chest of plate, box of linen, piano and similar handsome items may come from the bride's family.

Don't involve your groom in every decision. You may like to choose the household goods or schemes of decoration together ; but don't consult him over saucepans, pillows or blankets.

Don't choose a home next door to either set of parents. You will settle into married life far better alone together.

Don't find a house in an utterly strange neighbourhood. Your bride will be isolated till neighbours are satisfied as to her respectability.

Don't saddle yourself with a high rent, simply because your wife has been brought up in a big house. She is choosing you in exchange for the extra accommodation she is giving up—if she is the right sort of woman.

XIII.—*BANNS AND LEGAL FORMALITIES.*

Don't fail to note that while marriages in England may be religious or civil, both must be rendered valid by certain legal formalities.

Don't forget that a valid religious marriage can take place only in a church or chapel licensed by the bishop for such ceremonies.

Don't omit the reading of the banns, which must be published on three Sundays before the ceremony, in the parish or parishes where you or your intended live.

Don't delay your marriage longer than three months after the publication of the banns, or they must be republished or a licence procured.

Don't forget to appoint at least two witnesses in front of whom the marriage must be performed, and who will attest the signing of the register.

Don't scorn a civil contract, if you prefer, done by certificate or licence from the superintendent registrar of the district in which you have both lived. Your mutual declaration is brief, and you may furnish a ring.

Don't disregard making financial arrangements to safeguard your wife from ruin or poverty in the event of your death.

Don't avoid, if you have private means, settling a certain portion upon your wife. While you live, she should have the interest of this amount, and no control over the capital.

Don't ignore arrangements for disposal of any large landed estate or sums of money. After your decease, these are generally settled upon the first and other sons in tail male with cross remainders between them, and in default of male issue, among the daughters.

Don't dismiss the influence of your bride's dowry. This is of ancient origin and brings your wife respect, lessening the humiliation of her social and legal position.

XIV.—*PLANNING THE DAY.*

Don't fix upon the morning for the ceremony, without providing luncheon for the guests. Smart modern society, however, books a wedding at 2 o'clock or 2.30. This is followed by an informal reception with champagne, tea, ices, and light refreshments.

Don't sigh, as father of the bride, over the expenses of music and decoration of the church, the conveyances, and entertainments.

Don't miscalculate the supply of carriages to convey guests to and from the church. Each carriage and pair, with grey horses extra, will cost up to 15s., with a guinea for the bride's equipage. Drivers will expect a tip.

Don't omit the cost of the wedding-cake in your reckoning.   A large, elaborate cake may run up to £8, with the ornamental stand extra.

Don't skimp on refreshments if you are the bride's mother.   Arrange for a caterer unless you prefer to prepare sweetmeats at home.

Don't rule out entertaining the wedding party at an hotel or restaurant if you don't want your home turned upside down.   However, this is a less familiar setting for the bride's *adieu* to her old home life.

Don't discount help from other grown-up daughters in your home.   They should naturally take some portion of the work off your hands.

Don't fail, on the day before the event, to make a display of the wedding gifts in a room of their own. Place smaller offerings prominently, for the sake of the thought that prompted them.

Don't forget to organise belated presents, telegrams of congratulation, and other distractions as they arrive.

Don't neglect to see that the bride has proper food to sustain her through the day's proceedings. She should not feel faint at the altar.

Don't delay in dressing for the event. Everyone should be ready in good time.

XV.—*THE BRIDE.*

Don't expect fair weather on your wedding-day, but may you have the sunshine of joy in your heart!

Don't dress in haste. You are entering upon an eternal condition to be blessed by God. Respond to those high inspirations and holy desires that will descend on this great day of your life.

Don't discourage the soothing words of your mother, sister, or friend as they deck you in your bridal gown.

Don't succumb to nerves from the rush and excitement of the wedding morning, though you will be all the more attractive for some maidenly diffidence.

Don't permit fatigue and exhaustion to mar the beauty of your countenance. You must look your best and control your emotions. Look happy, for you are completing the choice you freely made.

Don't dress your hair to suit the veil rather than your face. Many girls wear their mother's bridal veil. The veil of a happy wife is supposed to bring good luck.

Don't adorn yourself with an excess of jewellery which seems vulgar on such a solemn occasion.

Don't rule out a simple prayer-book, borne in ungloved hands, in place of a bridal bouquet.

Don't fail to acknowledge those sacred moments when you are ready and the others have all started for the church.

Don't fail to savour the journey to church with your father, who will then bestow you upon your husband. It is the finest occasion in your lives together.

Don't fear if he is unable to accompany you to church. In this case, your mother will drive with you ; a close relation or friend will act as your father's deputy and meet you at the church door.

Don't stride triumphantly through your wedding. You will not show the best taste.

XVI.—*THE BRIDESMAIDS.*

Don't object to helping the hostess with preparations on the morning of the happy day. She may ask you to join in decorating the house with flowers, take messages and telegrams, and deal with other distractions.

Don't fuss in preparing yourself for the day. The bride will have chosen costumes for you and your companions that are comfortable and show both you and her at your best.

Don't dally at the church. You must await the bride, ready to follow her up the aisle.

Don't forget, as chief bridesmaid, to take the gloves and bouquet from the bride before she puts on the ring.

Don't disdain the groom or best man when they present you with a trinket or posy at the church. Your part in the day will make or mar your friend's joy.

Don't neglect to help the bride don her travelling costume as the time for departure draws near. Her sister, close friend, or mother will doubtless use this time to speak the real "Good-byes" before she rejoins the company.

XVII.—*THE GROOM AND BEST MAN.*

Don't sleep under the same roof as your *fiancée* the night before the wedding.

Don't see your beloved on the day, till you meet her in all her bridal beauty. Tradition asks her to retire even from her household early in the day; but more modern views now prevail.

Don't expect, as the groom, to receive as much attention as your bride. It is probably a matter of clothes.

Don't forget to have the ring ready, provide a conveyance to take yourself and the best man to the scene of the ceremony, and be punctual, waiting for the arrival of your bride.

Don't despair if you don't always feel quite happy or at ease under the eyes of the congregation. They will know it is only your modesty.

Don't neglect to present the bridesmaids with a small gift or posy, and a bouquet to your bride. Sometimes the best man gives flowers to each bridesmaid but it is generally the groom, unless you are all related.

Don't, as best man, consider it your duty to watch for the groom seeking to flee at the eleventh hour !

Don't ignore the etiquette of seating in the church. The brothers or cousins of the bride show the guests to their places. The groom's family and friends sit on the right, the bride's people on the left.

XVIII.—*THE RECEPTION.*

Don't mar the moment for the newly-weds by setting off too early from the church. Let them drive off first. They must be ready to greet the guests, on return to the house.

Don't expect much of the bride's attention, where there are many guests. She will have to divide her favours among the company.

Don't seat the bride for the meal elsewhere than between her husband and father. The newly-weds will take the head of the table or the centre of one side of the festive board.

Don't dread the boredom of long speeches. This practice has fallen into disuse.

Don't be constrained to conversation with one group at an informal reception. Here, you have the freedom to move about.

Don't permit anyone other than the bride to cut the cake. Each guest is invited to partake of it.

Don't be boisterous in your leave-taking of the departing couple.

Don't stay to the bitter end and pocket morsels of bridecake.

Don't poke about among the gifts unless in the company of one of the family or a bridesmaid ; there may be a detective present who might misinterpret friendly interest to the discomfort of a prying guest.

XIX.—*THE HONEYMOON.*

Don't show sorrow as you take leave of the assembled company, and they wish you God-speed. At this moment frivolous brothers and cousins may perform impish pranks, while you and your parents are feeling the keen pang of separation.

Don't throw rice at the young couple, which is not soothing to receive in the eye or ear. Paper confetti are a harmless substitute. Throwing old shoes is a relic from ancient times of the sticks and stones hurled by defeated friends when the victorious bridegroom carried off the bride as his prize and captive.

Don't reveal your newly married state on the wedding journey. Some couples take old portmanteaux to escape detection.

Don't hang your new husband round with bags, hat-boxes, and other impedimenta.

Don't force your bride, if she quickly feels fretted and looks jaded, or is physically indisposed by a long railway journey, to take her honeymoon far from home.

Don't oblige your beloved, if she is not reliably happy on board ship, to cross the water and end her wedding-day with *mal de mer*.

Don't over-extend your honeymoon. Men were made for something more virile than billing and cooing. When the sweetness begins to cloy, it is time to return to everyday life.

Don't forget that in courtship you are kept in check by your uncertain position. In matrimony, you see each other in all circumstances, both mentally trying and physically unbecoming.

Don't undervalue love and trust, common sense, humour, and a broad view of life. Where these are present, any possible disillusion should be but a passing cloud.

Don't disregard that the first year of married life will prove your union a failure or success. The end of the honeymoon signals the start of your real work together. You must each hold true through the dull days of ordinary life.

XX.—*THE NEWLY-MARRIED COUPLE IN SOCIETY.*

Don't reveal your home-coming to your circle by sending wedding-cards. This is outmoded. Cards should only be sent to old friends with wedding-cake.

Don't wait at home for callers. You may go out as you please. Return all calls made upon you in due time, and note the At Home days and addresses of your new acquaintances.

Don't delay in giving an At Home to friends who presented gifts, and to those who attended your wedding. Send out invitations in your name only ; your husband should put in an appearance if possible.

Don't welcome callers without wearing or using their gifts. Otherwise there should be no formal display of presents.

Don't start an acquaintance with older married people ; it is not your place.

Don't, as the new bride and guest of honour at a party, wear any colour but white. At a grand affair, you may wear a modified edition of your wedding gown.

Don't bore the company by quoting your new husband as a world-oracle. Civilised humanity has not been waiting through dark ages of perplexity for your recent domestic discoveries.

XXI.—*MARRIAGES REQUIRING FURTHER THOUGHT.*

Don't marry your first cousin. It is your plain duty to abstain from such a union as the intermarriage of family members leads to physical deterioration in unborn generations.

Don't marry where there is any hereditary disease of mind or body. It is little short of criminal to contract such a union.

Don't marry a European unless the man is cosmopolitan in his ideas or the woman can fit in with continental modes of life. A wife in England is held in higher regard than in any other country in Europe.

Don't marry a foreigner without strict observance of the marriage laws in his country. You might otherwise find yourself married in England but legally repudiated abroad.

Don't fail to settle the form of marriage ceremony if you and your beloved differ in religious faith and practice.

Don't be surprised if your bride gets her own way over the religious ceremony.

Don't marry a minor without the consent of parents. Scotch marriages at Gretna Green are no longer legally recognised.

XXII.—*SECOND MARRIAGES.*

Don't enter marriage a second time without recognising the compliment paid to your departed first spouse.

Don't forget Dr. Johnson's epigram : "The triumph of Hope over Experience."

Don't rule out that real romance may awaken only with your second wooing. It need be no mere prosaic, practical transaction.

Don't disregard the welfare of any children from your first marriage in your choice of husband or wife, especially the latter. A step-mother is often held in disfavour, probably because her relations with the young people are so intimate.

Don't ignore the romantic potential of a widow. She is familiar with both sexes, experienced, accessible, and versed in the lore of love.

Don't rush to buy a second engagement ring ; your lady may prefer some other trinket. She may wish to retain her first wedding-ring. If she decides to banish it, she should do so before marriage to you.

Don't choose grey for your widow's wedding frock. You may wear any light, delicate colour ; but a woman has only one *white* wedding and one bridal veil in her life.

Don't make a grand display over a second wedding, but cultivate an air of somewhat chastened joy.

Don't select a bouquet of purely white flowers; orange blossom is not permitted.

Don't eschew a second edition of the wedding cake and presents, but avoid favours and floral tributes.

Don't, if your new wife already has a nice home of her own, take up position as master of the household that has hitherto gone on quite well without you, without great tact and thought.

Don't rule out an entire change of servants; this is advisable, nay inevitable.

Don't fail to accord your new husband full dignity, and don't let it seem he is regarded as a pensioner on your bounty.

Don't disdain a speedy search for a nice new wife if yours dies, leaving you with young children, or even a baby. She will console you and mother the little ones.

Don't offer a home to a sister or niece as a permanency, to help if your wife dies. Be under no illusion that if you remarry, she is likely to need shelter elsewhere, having tided you over the worst part of your life.

Don't, if you have a house or estate, fail to consult your future spouse about any alterations you propose to undertake before your marriage.

Don't disregard etiquette. Even a widow requires a chaperone on her visits of inspection, either her mother, a married relation, or lady friend.

Don't expect to preside over your *fiancé*'s household till after your marriage if he has a grown-up daughter who is currently filling this rôle.

Don't take a second wife without informing any adult sons and daughters who may reside with you.

Don't install a step-mother over youths of her own age. This places them all in a difficult position, and may create tragedy.

Don't marry a spinster without considering a full smart wedding even on your second or third marriage. It is the condition of your bride that decides such matters.

Don't be alarmed at comparisons with No. 1 in thought if not in word, involuntarily if not intentionally. It is not generous of No. 2 to try and banish the memory of the dead.

Don't hope for an ideal companion for middle age if your new spouse lightly abandons all memories of the partner of youth. It is better to cherish a regard for the dead alongside an honest love for the living.

Published 2012 by A&C Black, an imprint of
Bloomsbury Publishing Plc
50 Bedford Square
London
WC1B 3DP

www.bloomsbury.com

Bloomsbury is a registered trademark of
Bloomsbury Publishing Plc

Copyright © Bloomsbury Publishing Plc, 2012

ISBN 9781408170847

A CIP catalogue record is available for this book
from the British Library.

Printed by WKT Company Ltd, China

5 7 9 10 8 6 4